AT THE FEET OF OUR ELDERS

A GUIDED JOURNAL OF 15 INTERVIEW QUESTIONS FOR CONVERSATIONS BETWEEN YOUNG CHILDREN AND THEIR ELDERS

THIS JOURNAL BELONGS TO

_____

Note to Parents:

This journal was designed to help facilitate conversations between young children and elders in their family or community. Each page has a space for children to draw a picture related to the discussion.

On one page there is a number one and on the opposing page there is a number two, indicating a space to interview two different elders. Elders can be grandparents, a neighbor, or someone else you know from the community. It's okay to help your child and it's okay to go at your own pace. This is a flexible experience that encourages communication and building relationships. Remember to have fun!

QUESTION

What was your favorite toy?

ELDER 1

WRITING SPACE

DRAWING

1

ELDER'S NAME:

ELDER'S RELATIONSHIP:

ELDER'S BIRTHDAY:

INTERVIEW DATE(S):

2

ELDER'S NAME:

ELDER'S RELATIONSHIP:

ELDER'S BIRTHDAY:

INTERVIEW DATE(S):

What was your favorite toy?

1

2

Why is your house far from my house?

1

What did you like about being parents to my parents?

1

2

What size was your house when you were little?

1

How did you learn the cool things you can do?
(planting, baking, sewing, card games, technology, fixing cars, etc)

1

What was school like when you were little and how did you get there every day?

1

2

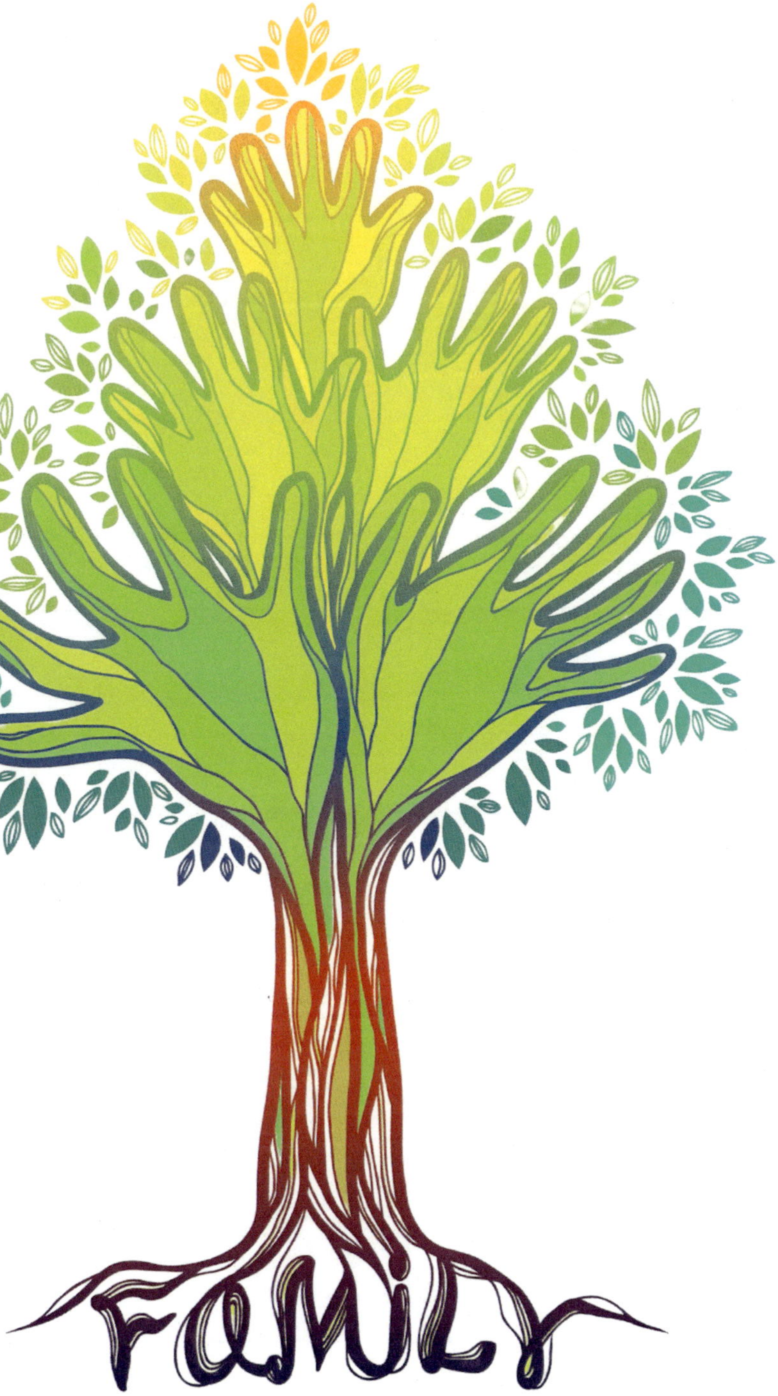
FAMILY

What games did you play when you were little?

1

What was your favorite book? What was it about?

1

Who was your hero?

1

What food did you like the most when you were little?

1

What food did you NOT like when you were little?

1

What did your family teach you how to do when you were a child?

1

Did you like to sing, dance or play an instrument?

1

Did you have a favorite show you liked to watch?

1

When you were my age, what did you want to be when you grew up?

1

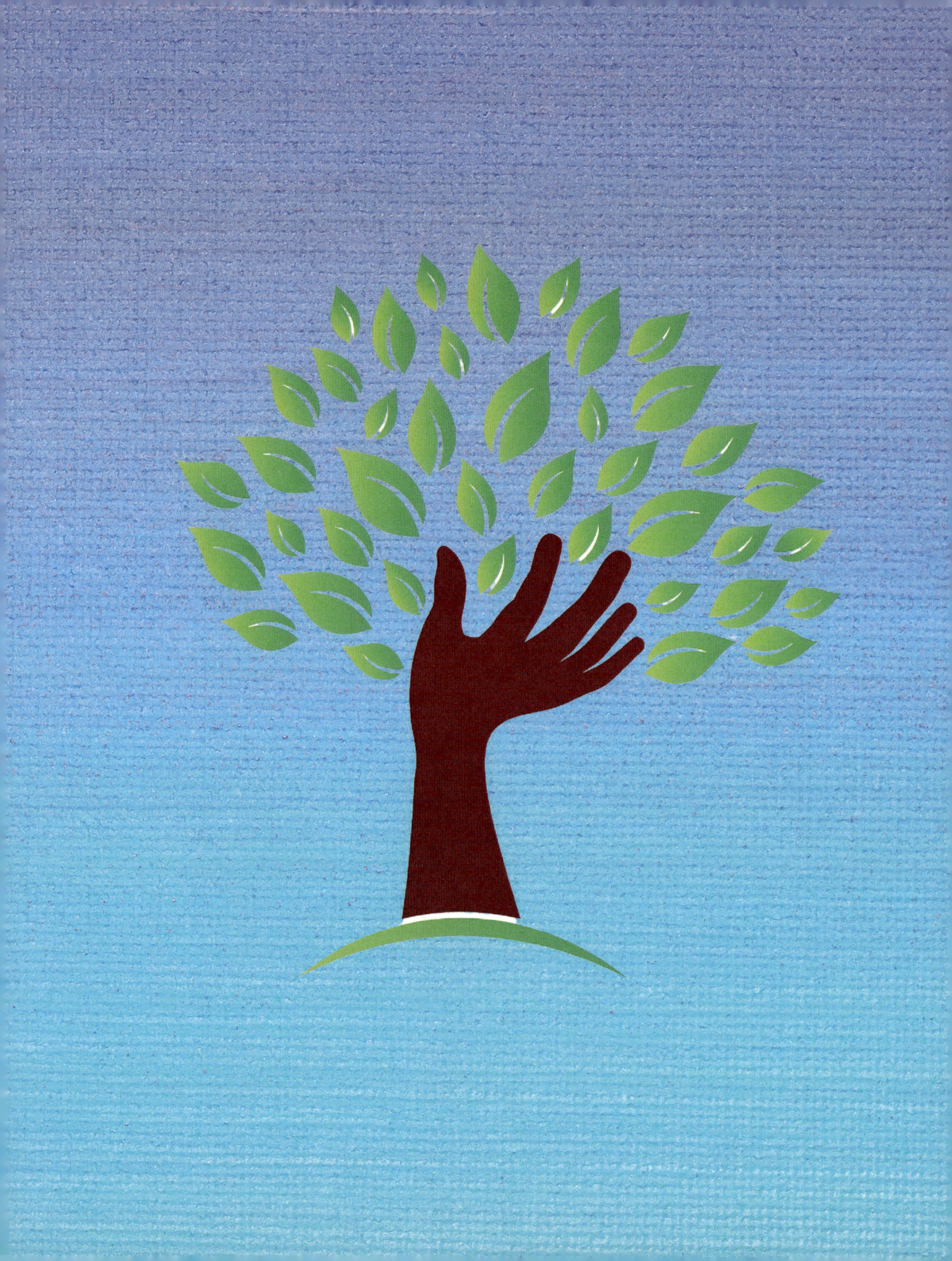

Free Write

You're doing a great job!

Use the next section to ask questions that are on your mind!

1

1

②

1

1

1

Copyright © 2020 Raise the Bar Learning, L.L.C.

At the Feet of Our Elders:
A Guided Journal of 15 Interview Questions for Conversations Between Young Children and Their Elders

Paperback

ISBN: 978-1-941592-21-2

All rights reserved.
No part of this work may be reproduced, transmitted, or stored in any form or by any means, including but not limited to photocopying, recording, scanning, digitizing, taping, web distribution information networks, or information storage or retrieval systems or any manner whatsoever without prior permission of the author, except where permitted by law.

Books may be purchased in quantity and/or special sales by contacting the publisher, Raise the Bar Learning, L.L.C. at www.raisethebarlearning.com

Printed in the United States of America

10 9 8 7 6 5 4 3 2 1

Made in the USA
Columbia, SC
23 February 2022